GETTING BY

P9-DHR-216

GERMAN

**A quick beginners' course for
tourists and businesspeople**

Course writer and producer: Edith Baer

Study booklet: Bryan Howson
Language Teaching Centre, University of York

Editor: Iris Sprankling

BARRON'S
Woodbury, New York / London / Toronto / Sydney

By arrangement with the British Broadcasting Corporation

First U.S. Edition published in 1982 by Barron's
Educational Series, Inc.

By arrangement with the British Broadcasting
Corporation, 35 Marylebone High Street, London
W1M 4AA.

All inquiries should be addressed to:
Barron's Educational Series, Inc.
113 Crossways Park Drive
Woodbury, New York 11797

International Standard Book No. 0-8120-2572-5

Library of Congress Cataloging in Publication Data
Baer, Edith, R.
Getting by in German.

Previously published as: Get by in German. 1981.
1. German language—Conversation and phrase
books.
2. German language—Grammar—1950-
I. Sprankling, Iris.   II. Title.
PF3121.B33   1982   438.3'421   82-8885
ISBN 0-8120-2572-5

PRINTED IN THE UNITED STATES OF AMERICA

45   550   9876543

2 zwei

Contents

The course... and how to use it

Getting by in German is a five-programme radio course for anyone planning to visit a German-speaking country. It has been designed to give you, in a short learning period, a basic 'survival kit' for some of the situations typical of a visit abroad.

'Getting by' means

- □ having a go at making yourself understood;
- □ listening for clues so that you can get the gist of what people say to you;
- □ knowing how to look up what you don't understand;
- □ knowing how to take short cuts;
- □ getting more fun out of your trip abroad.

Each programme

- ☐ is based on real-life conversations specially recorded in Germany so that you get used to hearing authentic everyday German right from the start;
- ☐ concentrates on the language you need to say and understand to cope with a particular situation, such as ordering food and drink, going shopping, booking in at a hotel;
- ☐ teaches you to speak the minimum you need to 'get by'—what you learn to speak has been chosen so that it's simple to say and useful in a variety of situations;
- ☐ gives you plenty of opportunities to repeat new words and expressions aloud in the pauses and to speak the answers to simple questions;
- ☐ helps you pick out the key information in what people say so that you can follow the general sense without worrying about the meaning of every word.

The cassettes

- ☐ contain the radio programmes in slightly shortened form;
- ☐ allow you to study at your own pace.

The study booklet includes

- ☐ the texts of the conversations heard in the programmes;
- ☐ a summary of what you need to say and listen out for;
- ☐ brief language explanations;
- ☐ self-checking exercises;
- ☐ tips about everyday life in Germany;
- ☐ tests to check if you can 'get by';
- ☐ a reference section containing a simple guide to pronunciation, a section on numbers, days of the week and months of the year, the answers to the exercises and a word list.

Have the study booklet (and a pencil) by you during the programmes. You'll sometimes be asked to write things down.

How to make the most of the course

Everyone has a personal way of learning and as you work through the course, you'll find the way best suited to you. Much will depend on whether you're using the cassettes or following the radio broadcasts, or both. Here are some suggestions:

☐ First get used to the sound of German by listening to the programme without looking at the book. If you're using the cassettes, you may prefer to go through the programme in sections. Before listening again, read through the book chapter.

☐ During the programme take every chance to get your tongue round the strange new sounds. Pronounce as boldly as you can the words and expressions you're asked to say. As well as helping you to get the sounds right, speaking aloud will make it easier for you to remember the words and phrases and give you confidence in speaking. On the cassettes the pauses for your replies are timed to allow for a little thought but a fairly prompt answer. If the pauses seem too short at first, lengthen them by stopping the tape. Continue practising until your answer fits the pause.

☐ After the programme work through the chapter in the study booklet. Read the conversations aloud — if possible with someone else. If you have the cassettes, check your pronunciation by imitating the speakers phrase by phrase (use the pause button to stop the tape). Go through the Language summary and Explanations, look up new words and phrases in the word list, do the exercises and read the notes about life in Germany. As with acquiring any other skill, learning a language needs frequent practice. A good rule is to do a little often. When you're on your own, driving to work or washing dishes, talk German to yourself or listen again to the cassette. If you have a friend or relative who is also following the course or who knows German, practise together. If something seems difficult the first time round, it will get easier the more you hear it.

☐ When you go abroad take this study booklet with you, plus a good pocket dictionary and a note book so that you can jot down the things you discover for yourself.

☐ At the end of the course go through the programmes and booklet again before working through the tests to see if you can 'get by'.

Can you 'GET BY'? (see page 56)
In these tests you are asked to remember most of the main language items in the course. Each test relates to one programme and book chapter. You can check your overall progress by working through all the tests together at the end of the course, or, if you prefer, you can test yourself as you go along, working through them one by one when you feel you have mastered the language in each programme.

If you can ' Get by in German ', you'll enjoy your visit all the more *Viel Spaß!*

1 Getting food and drink

Conversations

These are the texts of some of the real-life conversations you'll hear in the programme. After you've listened to the broadcast or cassette, read the conversations aloud as often as you can. If possible, practise them with someone else. If you have the cassette, use it to check your pronunciation.

Before attempting the conversations, you may prefer to go through the Language summary and Explanations on pages 12 and 13.

Native speakers will, of course, express themselves more eloquently than you need to. We have, therefore, printed in **bold letters** the minimum of language you need to be able to say to 'get by'.

Ordering breakfast

Im Hotel

Guest	**Guten Morgen!**
Waitress	Guten Morgen, Frau Müller. Möchten Sie frühstücken?
Guest	Oh **ja, bitte.**
Waitress	Kaffee oder Tee? Sie können auch gerne Schokolade haben.
Guest	**Tee, bitte.**
Waitress	Nehmen Sie mit Zitrone oder Sahne?
Guest	**Mit Zitrone, bitte.**

möchten Sie frühstücken? *would you like breakfast?*
Sie können auch gerne Schokolade haben *you can also have chocolate*
nehmen Sie mit Zitrone oder Sahne? *do you take it with lemon or cream?*

Ordering coffee and cakes

In der Konditorei

Waiter	Guten Tag! Bitte schön?

Customer	Ich möchte gerne **Kaffee** trinken.
Waiter	Ein Kännchen Kaffee? Eine Tasse Kaffee?
Customer	**Eine Tasse** Kaffee.

bitte schön? *yes please?*
ich möchte gerne Kaffee trinken *I'd like (to drink) coffee*
ein Kännchen Kaffee *a small pot of coffee*
eine Tasse Kaffee *a cup of coffee*

Waiter	Bitte schön?
Customer	**Zwei Tassen Kaffee, bitte.**
Waiter	Zwei Tassen Kaffee. Möchten Sie bitte Kuchen dazu? Obstkuchen, Käsekuchen, Bienenstich, Sahnetorte?
Customer	**Obstkuchen.**
Waiter	Obstkuchen.
Customer	*(to friend)* Möchten Sie auch **Obstkuchen?**
Friend	Ja, bitte.
Customer	**Bitte zwei Stück Obstkuchen.**
Waiter	Mit Sahne oder ohne Sahne?

möchten Sie bitte Kuchen dazu? *would you like cake with it?*
Käsekuchen *cheesecake*
Bienenstich *kind of honey and almond cake*
Sahnetorte *kind of cream gateau*
möchten Sie auch Obstkuchen? *would you like fruit tart as well?*
zwei Stück Obstkuchen *two pieces of fruit tart*

Ordering drinks

Im Restaurant

Waiter	Möchten Sie ein Glas Wein oder eine Flasche Wein?
Customer	**Zwei Glas Wein, bitte.**
Waiter	Zwei Glas Wein.

ein Glas Wein *a glass of wine*
eine Flasche Wein *a bottle of wine*

Waitress	Guten Abend!
Customer	Ein **Bier, bitte.**

Waitress	Ein großes* oder ein kleines?
Customer	**Ein großes** Bier.

*ß This letter is equivalent to ss

ein großes oder ein kleines? *a large or small (one)?*

Customer	Guten Abend! Ich möchte **bitte ein Bier.**
Waiter	Ein Bier? Ein kleines oder ein großes?
Customer	**Ein kleines, bitte.**

Ordering another drink

Customer	**Herr Ober,** bringen Sie bitte **noch ein Bier!**
Waiter	Bitte schön.

Customer	**Herr Ober!**
Waiter	Ja, bitte?
Customer	**Bitte noch zwei Bier.**
Waiter	Zwei Bier, jawohl.

Paying the bill

In der Konditorei

Customer	**Bitte zahlen!**
Waitress	Eine Tasse Kaffee, ein Apfelstrudel.
Customer	**Ja.**
Waitress	Drei Mark, bitte.
Customer	*(paying)* **Bitte** schön.
Waitress	Danke vielmals! Schönen Dank! Wiedersehen!
Customer	**Wiedersehen!**

danke vielmals! *many thanks*
schönen Dank! *thank you very much*

Customer	**Herr Ober, bitte zahlen!**
Waiter	Ja. Bitte schön. So, ein Kännchen Kaffee, eine Tasse Kaffee, ein Obstkuchen mit Sahne, ein Obstkuchen ohne Sahne. Sechs Mark achtzig, bitte schön.

Language summary

• WHAT YOU NEED TO SAY

How to say 'hello' . . .
Guten Tag! *any time of day*
Guten Morgen! *in the morning*
Guten Abend! *in the evening*

. . . and 'goodbye'
Auf Wiedersehen! *any time*
Wiedersehen! *more casual*

How to accept something . . .
Ja, bitte

. . . or refuse politely
Nein, danke

Ordering something to drink
Kaffee, bitte
Eine Tasse Kaffee
Ein Kännchen Kaffee

Tee, bitte
Tee mit Zitrone
Tee mit Sahne

Wein, bitte
Ein Glas Wein
Eine Flasche Wein

Bier, bitte
Ein kleines Bier
Ein großes Bier

Schokolade, bitte
Eine Tasse Schokolade

Ordering another drink
Noch ein Bier
Noch ein Kännchen

Ordering for two people
Zwei Tassen Kaffee
Zwei Glas Wein
Zwei Kännchen Tee
Zwei Stück Obstkuchen

Calling the waiter or waitress . . .
Herr Ober!
Fräulein!

. . . and asking for the bill
Zahlen, bitte!
Bitte zahlen!

Being asked what you want . . .	**. . . and how you want it**
Bitte schön?	Mit Zitrone oder Sahne?
Kaffee oder Tee?	Mit oder ohne Sahne?
Möchten Sie Kuchen dazu?	Ein kleines oder ein großes?

Explanations

In German, people and things are divided into three groups: masculine, feminine and neuter (marked m., f., n. in dictionaries).

There are three words for 'the': **der** (masculine), **die** (feminine), **das** (neuter). In the word list at the end of this booklet **der, die** and **das** are used instead of m., f., and n. When you learn a new word always try to learn it together with its **der, die** or **das,** like this:

der Kuchen   **die Tasse**   **das Bier**

Words with **ein** are masculine or neuter, words with **eine** are feminine:

ein Kuchen **(m)**		eine Tasse **(f)**
ein Bier **(n)**	but	eine Flasche **(f)**

You'll also come across **einen** which, said quickly, sounds nearly the same as **ein** . It's used with masculine words when you say what you want, have, are taking, and so on: **Möchten Sie einen Kaffee?**

Nouns in German are written with a capital letter: **Kaffee oder Tee?** So is **Sie** when it means 'you': **Nehmen Sie mit Zitrone oder Sahne?**

An *Umlaut* (marked by two dots over a vowel) changes the vowel's sound. Pay particular attention to *Umlaut* vowels when you're listening to the recordings or imitating the speakers.

ß is sometimes used instead of 'ss': **Ein kleines oder ein großes?** (See p 63)

Numbers are important for 'getting by'. You need them for coping with prices, fares, times, bus numbers, phone numbers, paying the bill, asking for your room key, etc.:

1	**eins**	6	**sechs**
2	**zwei**	7	**sieben**
3	**drei**	8	**acht**
4	**vier**	9	**neun**
5	**fünf**	10	**zehn**

People often use **zwo** instead of **zwei** when quoting prices, times, phone numbers, and so on. This is to avoid confusion with **drei**.

Exercises

1 What do you say? Choose from the three alternatives.

It's one o'clock. You meet a friend and greet him.

What do you say?   Guten Abend!
                 Auf Wiedersehen!
Guten Tag   Guten Tag!

You go to a restaurant together. You're offered beer, which you don't fancy.

What do you say?   Zwei Bier, bitte.
Nein, danke   Nein, danke.
                 Mit Zitrone.

Your friend sticks to beer, but you'd like a little wine.

What do you say?   Ein kleines.
                 Eine Flasche Wein.
Ein glas Wein   Ein Glas Wein.

After lunch you order two cups of coffee.

What do you say?   Ein Kännchen Kaffee.
                 Zwei Glas Kaffee.
Zwei Tassen Kaffee   Zwei Tassen Kaffee.

The waiter suggests cake as well. But you've had enough to eat.

What do you say? Ja, bitte.
Nein, danke. Nein, danke.
  Mit Sahne.

2 You're in a café.
Where's the waitress? Call her. *Fräulein*!
Ask her for a cup of coffee. *eine Tasse Kaffee, bitte*
With cream. *mit Sahne.*
And then another cup of coffee. *noch eine Kaffee*
Call her again and ask for the bill. *Fräulein, bitte, Zahlen*!

3 Now it's drinks all round.
Call the waiter. *Herr Ober*!
Order a beer for yourself. *ein Bier, bitte*
A friend comes to join you. Order another beer.
noch ein Bier, bitte

Then a couple you know joins you. She'd like a cup of coffee, he wants a glass of wine.
eine Tasse Kaffee und ein Glas Wein

Later two business friends turn up with their wives. One lady would like a cup of coffee, the other a small pot of tea. The men want wine — better order a bottle.
eine Tasse Kaffee und ein Kännchen Tee und eine Flasche Wein, bitte

It's time to pay. Call the waiter and ask for the bill.
Herr Ober, bitte Zahlen

The waiter is confused and says: 'Ein Bier, eine Tasse Kaffee, ein Glas Wein, ein Kännchen Kaffee, ein Glas Tee.' Correct him saying what you did have.

....

....

4 What's the answer here?

acht Tassen Kaffee und zwei Tassen Kaffee = ... *10 cups coffee ...... Zehn Tassen Kaffee*

drei Glas Wein und fünf Glas Wein = *8 glasses wine*

vier Bier und zwei Bier = *6 beers Acht Bier*

fünf Tee und ein Tee = ... *6 tee , Sech Tee*

5 What do you make of these questions?
Choose the right answer.

Möchten Sie Kuchen?

Are you being	a	offered a drink?
	✓ b	asked if you want cake?
	c	asked if you want breakfast?

Bitte schön?

Are you being	✓ a	asked for your order?
	b	thanked for your help?
	c	offered a cigarette?

Ein großes oder ein kleines?

Are you being asked	a	if you'd like two beers?
	b	if you'd like another beer?
	✓ c	what size beer you'd like?

It's worth knowing

Greetings

In German-speaking countries people tend to say
'hello' and goodbye' more than we do, for example,
when entering or leaving a shop, a small restaurant, a
hotel dining-room, a train compartment. In Southern
Germany and Austria you'll hear people saying **Grüß
Gott!** instead of **Guten Tag!** and **Auf Wiedersehen!**

Addressing people

It's polite to call a man **Herr . . .**, a married or not so
young woman **Frau . . .**, a young woman or girl
Fräulein . . . followed by their surname. **Fräulein** on
its own is used to call the waitress. Address the
waiter as **Herr Ober.**

Saying please and thank you

You'll hear a variety of ways of saying thank you: **danke schön, danke vielmals, schönen Dank, herzlichen Dank, ich danke auch.** It's enough for you to say **danke.** In reply to an offer, **danke** is sometimes taken to mean 'no thank you', so if you want to accept, say **ja, bitte. Bitte** or **bitte schön** can mean 'please', or be a polite reply to **danke schön.** People in shops, restaurants, etc. say **Bitte schön?** to ask you what you want.

Food and drink

Most hotels serve a set 'continental breakfast' consisting of tea or coffee, bread or rolls, butter and jam. You're sometimes offered cheese (**Käse**) or sliced sausage (**Wurst**). A soft-boiled egg (**ein weichgekochtes Ei**) is usually extra.

If you're in a restaurant and want the menu ask for *this* die Speisekarte or die Karte. If you can't make out *card* what the various dishes are, ask for a set meal (**Gedeck** or **Menü.**) It's often the best buy. You may hear the waiter say **einmal, zweimal,** etc. as he notes down your order: **einmal Menü eins, zweimal Obstkuchen mit Sahne** (one set meal No. 1, two fruit tarts with cream). You can also use **einmal, zweimal,** etc. when ordering. Restaurant charges normally include service, but it's common practice to give a small tip by rounding up the amount to the nearest **Mark** (in Germany) or **Franken** (in Switzerland) and saying **stimmt so**—keep the change. In Austria you add about 10%. Many restaurants and cafés are closed one day a week. The sign **Ruhetag** (rest day) tells you.

Germany is well known for its beer and the choice is vast. You can buy it draught, i.e. from the barrel (**vom Faß**) or you can buy a bottle (**eine Flasche**), which is often more expensive.

Coffee is automatically served with cream, not milk. You can order a cup (**eine Tasse**) or you can ask for **ein Kännchen,** a small pot for one.

2 Getting your shopping done

Note: Prices, of course, are constantly changing. Be prepared for different prices from those in the recordings when you visit Germany!

Conversations

In der Drogerie (*chemist's*)

Assistant	Guten Tag! Was wünschen Sie, bitte?
Customer	Ja, **guten Tag! Puder, bitte.**

was wünschen Sie? *what would you like?*

Am Kiosk

Assistant	Guten Tag! Bitte schön?
Customer	**Guten Tag!** Haben Sie **Postkarten?**
Assistant	Nein. Die haben wir leider nicht.
Customer	Und **englische Zigaretten?**
Assistant	Die haben wir auch leider nicht.* *(also)*

*In everyday language people sometimes speak colloquially. Standard German word order would be: **Die haben wir leider auch nicht.**

die haben wir leider (auch) nicht *I'm afraid we don't have them (either)*

Customer	Haben Sie **Postkarten?**
Assistant	Ja.
Customer	Ah, ja. *(pointing at one)* **Die da.**
Assistant	Ja.
Customer	**Was kostet die?**
Assistant	Fünfzig Pfennige. *50*
Customer	**Zwei** Stück, **bitte.** Haben Sie auch **Briefmarken?**
Assistant	Ja.

Customer	Was kostet **eine Postkarte nach England?**
Assistant	Fünfzig Pfennige.
Customer	Ja. **Zwei Briefmarken** für England. . .

(to) *(for)*

Beginning of side two, cassette one

Customer	. . . Haben Sie **englische Zigaretten?**
Assistant	Zwo siebzig oder zwo fünfundachtzig.
Customer	**Zwei siebzig, bitte.** Und haben Sie **Streichhölzer?*** matches
Assistant	Ja. Die haben wir auch.

*These cost **siebzig Pfennig** — you'll need to know this in Exercise 6.

haben Sie (auch) . . .? *have you (also) . . .?*
die da *that one*
was kostet die? *how much is that one?*
zwei Stück *two of them*
die haben wir auch *we have those too*
those we

Im Postamt *(post office)*

Customer	Was kostet **ein Brief nach England?**
Clerk	Siebzig Pfennige.
Customer	Und **eine Postkarte?**
Clerk	Eine Postkarte kostet fünfzig Pfennige.
Customer	**Drei** Briefmarken **zu siebzig** und **fünf** Briefmarken **zu fünfzig.**
Clerk	Drei Briefmarken zu siebzig und fünf Briefmarken zu fünfzig. Das macht zwei Mark fünfzig und zwei Mark zehn. Das sind zusammen vier Mark und sechzig.

zu siebzig *at 70* zu fünfzig *at 50*
das macht *that comes to* das sind zusammen *altogether that's*

In der Drogerie

Assistant	Guten Tag! Was wünschen Sie, bitte?

Customer	**Guten Tag! Pflaster, bitte.**
Assistant	Eine große Packung oder eine kleine Packung?
Customer	**Eine kleine.***
Assistant	Haben Sie sonst noch einen Wunsch?
Customer	**Ja, bitte. Puder.** *powder*
Assistant	Eine Mark zehn. Sonst noch einen Wunsch?
Customer	Haben Sie **Zahnkrem?** *cream*
Assistant	Ja. Die große Packung zu fünf Mark dreißig oder die kleine Packung zu zwo fünfundneunzig.
Customer	Oh, **die da. Die kleine.**
Assistant	Die kleine. Haben Sie sonst noch einen Wunsch?
Customer	**Nein, danke.** Das ist alles.
Assistant	Möchten Sie eine Tüte?
Customer	Oh **ja, bitte.** *(bag)*

*This costs **eine Mark zwanzig.**
haben Sie sonst noch einen Wunsch? *would you like anything else?*
das ist alles *that's all*

An der Tankstelle *(petrol station)*

Attendant	Guten Tag! Was möchten Sie, bitte?
Customer	**Guten Tag! Für zehn Mark, bitte.**
Attendant	Super oder Normal?
Customer	**Normal, bitte.**
Attendant	Normal.

für zehn Mark *ten marks' worth*

Attendant	Guten Tag!
Customer	**Guten Tag!**
Attendant	Super oder Normal?
Customer	**Super voll, bitte.**
Attendant	Voll, ja. Gut.
Customer	**Was macht das?**
Attendant	Dreiundzwanzig Mark siebzig. *23 m 70 ₰*
Customer	*(paying)* **Bitte** schön.

| *Attendant* | Danke schön. Wiedersehen! Gute Fahrt! |

voll, bitte *fill her up*
gute Fahrt! *have a good trip!*

Language summary

● WHAT YOU NEED TO SAY

Saying what you want . . .

Zigaretten, bitte
Zwei Briefmarken für England
Drei zu siebzig
Die kleine Packung
Super, bitte
Voll, bitte
Für zehn Mark

. . . and asking how much it is

Was macht das?
Was kostet die?
Was kostet eine Postkarte?
Was kostet ein Brief nach England?

What to say if you don't understand

Wie bitte?
Langsam, bitte

● WHAT YOU NEED TO LISTEN OUT FOR

Being asked what you want

Bitte schön?
Was wünschen Sie, bitte?
(Haben Sie) sonst noch einen Wunsch? *another*

Being told they haven't got it

Die haben wir leider nicht
Die haben wir leider auch nicht

sorry
unfortunately
also

Explanations

You may have noticed these differences:

| eine Tasse | but | zwei Tassen |
| eine Briefmarke | but | drei Briefmarken |

Many words add 'n' in the plural. Others add 'e', 'er', 'en' or 's'. Some stay the same. Some add an *Umlaut*. There are no easy rules about this. The best thing is to learn the plurals as you come across them. What you add to a word to make its plural is indicated in the word list and in dictionaries in brackets, like this:

der Brief (-e)   der Kuchen (-)
der Herr (-en)   das Streichholz (¨er)
das Hotel (-s)   die Tasse (-n)

In the plural the word for 'the' is **die**. So the plurals of the above words are:

die Brief**e**   die Kuchen
die Herr**en**   die Streichhölz**er**
die Hotel**s**   die Tass**en**

You say eine groß**e** Packung but ein klein**es** Bier. That's because **Packung** is a word with **die** and **Bier** a word with **das**.

Some more numbers:

20	**zwanzig**	30	**dreißig**
21	**einundzwanzig**	31	**einunddreißig**
22	**zweiundzwanzig**	40	**vierzig**
23	**dreiundzwanzig**	50	**fünfzig**
24	**vierundzwanzig**	60	**sechzig**
25	**fünfundzwanzig**	70	**siebzig**
26	**sechsundzwanzig**	80	**achtzig**
27	**siebenundzwanzig**	90	**neunzig**
28	**achtundzwanzig**	100	**hundert**
29	**neunundzwanzig**	200	**zweihundert**

The tens all end in -**zig**, except drei**ß**ig. Numbers above twenty start with **ein**-, **zwei**-, **drei**- . . . followed by **und** and the tens, like the English five-and-twenty: **fünfundzwanzig**. Numbers are written as one word.

Exercises

1 You haven't much German money left, so choose the cheaper of the things offered:

Möchten Sie die Zigaretten zu zwei achtzig oder zu zwei fünfzig? *Zwei fünfzig*

Möchten Sie eine kleine Flasche Kölnisch Wasser *(Eau de Cologne)* zu fünf Mark dreißig oder die Flasche zu neun Mark fünfzig? *fünf Mark dreißig*

Nehmen Sie die Postkarten zu fünfzig oder die Postkarten zu fünfundfünfzig? *fünfzig*

Was möchten Sie? Eine große Packung Zahnkrem oder eine kleine? *eine kleine*

Möchten Sie fünf Briefmarken oder zehn? *fünf Briefmarken*

Was möchten Sie? Eine Tasse Kaffee oder ein Kännchen? *Eine Tasse Kaffee*

Möchten Sie ein Stück Kuchen oder zwei? *ein stück Kuchen*

Super oder Normal? *Normal*

2 You're shopping. The shop assistant says:

Was wünschen Sie?

Are you being   (a) asked what you want?

         b   asked if you want anything else?

         c   asked which size you want?

Sonst noch einen Wunsch?

Are you being   a   offered a plastic bag?

         (b) asked what else you want?

         c   asked if you're being served?

Möchten Sie eine Tüte?

Are you being   a told what your bill comes to?
                     b asked if you want anything
                           else?
                    (c) offered a bag for your
                           shopping?

3 How do you ask what the bill comes to?

Was macht das ?

You want to point out which postcard you like

die da

and know how much it is. *was kostet die* ?

You want to buy a bottle of wine. *eine flasche wein*

and know how much a bottle costs. *was kostet eine wein* ?

You ask for two bottles. *zwei flaschen wein bitte*

4 You're in the chemist's buying some things you've
forgotten to bring with you. You've looked up the
words for what you want in the dictionary:

soap — Seife (f)
toothbrush — Zahnbürste (f)

Fill in your side of the conversation. The words in
brackets tell you what to say.

Assistant   Guten Tag! Bitte schön?
You   (Greet her and ask for soap)
    Guten Tag!, Seife, bitte
Assistant   Ja. Möchten Sie die Seife hier zu
                achtzig oder die da zu fünfzig?
You   (Take the more expensive one)
    Die Seife zu Achtzig
Assistant   Haben Sie sonst noch einen Wunsch?
You   (You want a toothbrush) *Ja,*
    eine Zahnbürste, bitte

Assistant	Ja. Möchten Sie die da?
You	(Say yes please, and ask how much it is.) *Ja, bitte. Was kostet die*
Assistant	Drei Mark. Sonst noch einen Wunsch?
You	(Toothpaste) *Ja, Zahnkrem bitte,*
Assistant	Die große oder die kleine Packung?
You	(Take the small one) *die kleine packung*
Assistant	Sonst noch einen Wunsch?
You	(Say no thank you, and ask how much it comes to) *Nein, danke, Was macht das?*
Assistant	Das macht sechs Mark fünfundvierzig. Möchten Sie eine Tüte? *6.45*
You	(Accept politely) *Ja, Bitte*

5 Here's your shopping list for the tobacconist's and the chemist's. Write in the prices. You'll find them in the conversations. Work out the total in German.

DM = Deutschmark

2 Postcards	
2 Stamps for postcards	1,00 DM
Cigarettes	DM
Matches	DM
Sticking plaster	DM
Powder	DM
Toothpaste	DM
Total	DM
	DM

6 The shop assistant makes out your bill. Check the total. If it isn't correct, put the right amount here:

....

....

Zigaretten—zwei Mark; Streichhölzer fünfundsechzig Pfennig; Puder-drei Mark; sechs Postkarten zu sechzig-drei Mark sechzig; drei Postkarten zu fünfzig—eine Mark fünfzig; zehn Briefmarken zu fünfzig—fünf Mark; eine Flasche Rheinwein-sieben Mark dreißig. Das macht dreiundzwanzig Mark fünfundsiebzig Pfennig.

It's worth knowing

Shops

In Germany and Austria most shops are open from eight or nine in the morning until half-past six at night. The smaller ones are closed between one and three. On Saturdays shops are closed in the afternoon, except on the first Saturday in every month when they're open until six.

In Switzerland shopping hours are similar. Shops usually close for one half day each week which varies with the locality. In some resorts in the high season you'll find shops open even on Sundays. If you see **geschlossen** on the door it means they're closed. Post offices are generally open from eight until six, but some close between twelve and two.

The posthorn, symbol of the German Federal Mail

Eine Drogerie is where you buy soap, cosmetics, toothpaste, etc. but not medicines. For those you have to go to **eine Apotheke.**

Buying petrol

If you want your tank filled, say **voll** or **volltanken,** otherwise buy your petrol in litres (**zehn Liter, bitte**) or so many mark's worth (**Super für zehn Mark,**

bitte). The two grades are **Super** (premium) and
Normal (regular). One gallon is about five litres.
You tip the attendant a small amount by rounding
up the sum to the next **Mark** or **Franken.**
Selbsttanken or **sb,** which stands for
Selbstbedienung, means you serve yourself.

German, Swiss and Austrian money

The **Mark** is the unit of currency in Germany. In
West Germany it's the **Deutschmark (DM),** in East
Germany the **Mark (M).** There are 100 **Pfennige
(Pf.)** to the mark.

In Switzerland, where 65% of the population is
German-speaking, the unit of currency is the **Franken
(Fr.).** The **Franken** has 100 **centimes,** referred to by
German speakers as **Rappen.**

In Austria the unit of currency is the **Schilling,**
which is made up of 100 **Groschen.**

3 Getting a hotel room

Conversations

Looking for a hotel

Tourist	Ist hier **ein Hotel?**
Passer-by	500 Meter weiter auf der rechten Seite finden Sie ein Hotel. Es ist ein Hotel garni.

auf der rechten Seite   *on the right-hand side*
ein Hotel garni   *bed and breakfast hotel*

Asking for a room

Guest	**Guten Tag!**
Receptionist	Guten Tag!
Guest	Haben Sie **ein Zimmer** frei?
Receptionist	Ja, gerne.
Guest	Ich möchte **ein Doppelzimmer.**

haben Sie ein Zimmer frei?   *have you a room (free)?*

Receptionist	Guten Tag!
Guest	**Guten Tag!** Haben Sie **ein Zimmer** frei?
Receptionist	Was hätten Sie denn gerne?
Guest	**Ein Einzelzimmer.**
Receptionist	Ein Zimmer mit oder ohne Dusche?
Guest	**Was kostet ein Zimmer mit Dusche?**
Receptionist	Mit Dusche achtunddreißig Mark und ohne Dusche dreißig Mark.
Guest	Aha. Ist das **mit Frühstück?**
Receptionist	Nein. Das Frühstück kostet fünf Mark extra.

was hätten Sie denn gerne?   *what would you like?*

Guest	**Guten Abend!** Haben Sie **ein Zimmer** frei, bitte?

Receptionist	Ja. Möchten Sie ein Einzelzimmer oder ein Doppelzimmer?
Guest	**Ein Einzelzimmer, bitte.**
Receptionist	Mit Dusche? Ohne Dusche? Oder mit Bad?
Guest	**Was kostet ein Zimmer mit Dusche?**
Receptionist	Vierzig oder fündundvierzig.
Guest	Und **ohne Dusche?**
Receptionist	Fünfunddreißig.
Guest	Ist das **mit oder ohne Frühstück?**
Receptionist	Mit Frühstück.

Phoning for breakfast

Guest	*(phoning)* **Frühstück, bitte.**
Receptionist	Kaffee oder Tee?
Guest	**Tee, bitte.**
Receptionist	Mit Zitrone oder Sahne?
Guest	**Mit Zitrone, bitte.**
Receptionist	Möchten Sie auch gerne ein Ei?
Guest	Ja. **Vier Minuten, bitte.**
Receptionist	Gerne.

Beginning of side 1, cassette two.

Asking for your key

Guest	**Guten Abend! Mein Schlüssel, bitte.**
Receptionist	Zimmer Nummer?
Guest	Zimmer Nummer **neunzehn.**
Receptionist	*(handing him the key)* Bitte schön. Ihr Schlüssel. Zimmer neunzehn.
Guest	**Danke.**

When there's no room available

| Guest | Haben Sie **ein Zimmer** frei? |
| Receptionist | Leider nein. Wir haben kein Zimmer mehr frei. |

wir haben kein Zimmer mehr frei *we've no more rooms available*

Receptionist	Guten Tag!
Guest	**Guten Tag!** Ich möchte gern **ein Doppelzimmer für zwei Nächte.**
Receptionist	Oh, für zwei Nächte, das tut mir leid. Wir sind leider voll ausgebucht.

für zwei Nächte *for two nights*
das tut mir leid *I'm sorry*
wir sind voll ausgebucht *we're fully booked*

| Guest | **Guten Abend!** Haben Sie **ein Zimmer** frei, **bitte?** |
| Receptionist | Guten Abend! Leider sind wir besetzt. |

leider sind wir besetzt *I'm afraid we're full*

Answering the phone . . .

Jürgen	*(answering phone)* **Andersen. Ja, bitte?**
Receptionist	Guten Morgen! Sieben Uhr.
Jürgen	**Danke.**
Receptionist	Möchten Sie frühstücken?
Jürgen	**Ja, bitte.**

Gabi	*(answering phone)* **Englet. Ja, bitte?**
Waiter	Guten Morgen, Frau Englet. Acht Uhr. Möchten Sie das Frühstück?
Gabi	**Ja, bitte.**
Waiter	Tee oder Kaffee?
Gabi	Nein. **Schokolade, bitte.**

. . . and making a call

| Jürgen | *(phoning)* **Hier Andersen. Ah, guten Tag, Herr Meyer.** |

| Jürgen | *(phoning)* **Guten Tag! Andersen** ist mein Name. **Herr Meyer, bitte.** |
| Telephonist | Ja, einen Moment, ich verbinde Sie. |

ich verbinde Sie *I'll put you through*

| Jürgen | *(phoning)* **Guten Tag! Andersen** ist mein Name. **Herr Meyer, bitte.** |

Secretary   Herr Meyer ist leider im Moment
               nicht da.*

*Standard word order would be be: . . . **ist im Moment leider
nicht da.**

. . . ist im Moment leider nicht da   . . . *isn't in at the moment
I'm afraid*

Language summary

● WHAT YOU NEED TO SAY

Asking for a room
Ein Zimmer, bitte
Ein Einzelzimmer
Ein Doppelzimmer
Mit Bad
Mit Dusche
Ohne Dusche

Asking the price
Was kostet das?
Mit Frühstück?

Asking for your key
Mein Schlüssel, bitte
Zimmer Nummer drei

● WHAT YOU NEED TO LISTEN OUT FOR

Being asked for your name
Ihr Name, bitte?
Wie ist Ihr Name?

Being asked how long you're staying
Für wie lange?
Für eine Nacht?
Für zwei Nächte?
Für drei Tage?

Being told there's no room
Leider nein
Wir haben kein Zimmer
   mehr frei
Wir sind besetzt
Wir sind ausgebucht

Explanations

In this programme you hear the words for 'my' **mein** and 'your' **Ihr**:

mein Schlüssel   **Ihr** Name

If the word is feminine, you say:

mein**e** Nummer   Ihr**e** Nummer

More numbers:

11	**elf**	16	**sechzehn**
12	**zwölf**	17	**siebzehn**
13	**dreizehn**	18	**achtzehn**
14	**vierzehn**	19	**neunzehn**
15	**fünfzehn**	20	**zwanzig**

Exercises

1 You and your wife/husband haven't much German money left, and you want a room (with breakfast) for the night. You enquire in several hotels and they all have rooms free. Below is what the receptionist in each hotel tells you. Which hotel offers the best value for your money?

Hotel Falkenstein: Ja, wir haben zwei Einzelzimmer mit Dusche frei. Ein Einzelzimmer kostet vierzig Mark, mit Frühstück.

Hotel Erlkönig: Ja, wir haben ein Doppelzimmer mit Dusche. Das kostet einhundertsechzig Mark mit Frühstück.

Hotel Cosmos: Ein Doppelzimmer ohne Dusche kostet siebenundfünfzig Mark. Das Frühstück ist extra—fünf Mark pro Person.

Now read what the hotels serve for breakfast. Which is the best breakfast?

Hotel Falkenstein: Kaffee, Brötchen, Butter, Gelée, Käse oder Wurst, ein Ei und Orangensaft.

Hotel Erlkönig: Zum Frühstück gibt's Tee oder Kaffee, Brötchen, Brot, Konfitüre, ein Ei.

Hotel Cosmos: Wir servieren Brötchen, Schwarzbrot, Butter, Marmelade und auch Käse oder Wurst.

2 What do you say? Choose the answer from the three alternatives.

You want a single room for one night.

What do you say?	Ein Doppelzimmer für eine Nacht.
.... ✓	Ein Einzelzimmer, für eine Nacht.
....	Mein Schlüssel, bitte. Zimmer einundzwanzig.

You want to know if the price quoted for a room includes breakfast.

What do you say? ✓	Ist das mit Frühstück?
....	Was kostet ein Zimmer mit Dusche?
....	Frühstück, bitte.

You and your wife/husband want a room with a shower.

What do you say?	Zwei Einzelzimmer, bitte.
....	Ein Doppelzimmer ohne Dusche, bitte.
.... ✓	Ein Doppelzimmer mit Dusche, bitte.

At breakfast you want to order lemon tea.

What do you say?	Tee mit Sahne, bitte.
.... ✓	Tee mit Zitrone, bitte.
....	Ist das mit Frühstück?

3 You arrive at a hotel in the evening and have this conversation with the receptionist. Fill in what you say.

Receptionist	Guten Abend! Was wünschen Sie?
You	(Greet her and ask for a room)

....

Receptionist	Für eine Person?
You	(No, you want a double room)............

....

Receptionist	Mit oder ohne Bad?
You	(You want a room with bath)............

....

Receptionist	Moment, bitte . . . Ja, wir haben ein Doppelzimmer frei.
You	(Better ask what the room costs)

....?

Receptionist	Vierzig Mark pro Tag.
You	(Find out if that includes breakfast)

....?

Receptionist	Nein, das Frühstück ist extra. Nehmen Sie das Zimmer?
You	(Yes, you will, please)...................
Receptionist	Gut. Ihr Name, bitte?
You	(Tell her your name)...................
Receptionist	Und wie lange bleiben Sie?
You	(You don't understand that)............

....?

Receptionist	Für eine Nacht?
You	(Yes, for one night)...................

....

It's worth knowing

In Germany and Switzerland there's no official classification of hotels. In Austria hotels are categorised as A1 (luxury), A, B, C, and D. Everywhere there are wide variations in standards and price. You're usually charged per room and not per person. Check to see if the price you're quoted includes breakfast. If you're told: **Ja, mit Frühstück und Mehrwertsteuer,** it includes VAT as well. ("Value-added tax" is a tax added at each stage of production of a consumer product, from raw material to finished product, as the item "grows in value" at each step.)

If the hotel is a **Hotel garni,** there will be no meals served except for breakfast and possibly snacks and drinks.

It's worth getting an up-to-date hotel list from the National Tourist Office of the country concerned for the area you wish to visit:

German National Tourist Office, 630 Fifth Avenue, Suite 1418, New York, NY 10020

The Swiss Center, 608 Fifth Avenue, New York, NY 10020

Austrian Information Service, 31 East 69th Street, New York, NY 10021

Using the phone

Answering the phone you say **Ja, bitte?** or **Guten Tag!** and your surname. Ringing someone up, you say **Guten Tag!** and your name followed by the name of the person you want to speak to: **Frau Meyer, bitte.** You may then hear: **Moment, bitte, ich verbinde Sie**—just a moment, please, I'll put you through. If the number's engaged you'll be told: **Die Nummer ist besetzt.**

If you call the speaking clock, you'll hear, for instance: **Beim nächsten Ton ist es elf Uhr vier Minuten and fünfzig Sekunden**—at the next stroke it will be eleven four and fifty seconds.

4 Getting about

Conversations

Asking someone for information

Tourist	**Entschuldigen Sie,** ist das der Zug **nach Hamburg,** bitte?
	Entschuldigen Sie bitte, wie komme ich **zum Bahnhof?**
	Entschuldigen Sie bitte, welcher Bus fährt **nach Altencelle?**

entschuldigen Sie *excuse me*
wie komme ich . . . ? *how do I get . . .?*
welcher Bus fährt nach Altencelle? *which bus goes to Altencelle?*

Paying for a taxi

Passenger	**Was macht das?**
Driver	Drei Mark, bitte.
Passenger	*(paying)* **Bitte. Stimmt so.**
Driver	Schönen Dank!
Passenger	**Was macht das, bitte?**
Driver	Ja, dann macht das vier Mark und zwanzig Pfennig.
Passenger	Vier Mark zwanzig. *(paying)* **Es stimmt** schon **so. Danke schön.**
Driver	**Bitte** sehr.
Passenger	Wiedersehen!
Driver	**Auf Wiedersehen!**
Passenger	**Was macht das?**
Driver	Das macht achtzehn Mark und sechzig Pfennig.
Passenger	*(paying)* **Es stimmt** schon **so.**
Driver	Danke schön.

Passenger	Was kostet die Fahrt **zum Flughafen?**
Driver	Zum Flughafen? Fünfundzwanzig bis dreißig Mark.

(es) stimmt (schon) so *keep the change*
fünfundzwanzig bis dreißig *twenty-five to thirty*

Being given information about bus and tram routes

Tourist	**Entschuldigen Sie bitte,** welcher Bus fährt **nach Altencelle?**
Passer-by	Nach Altencelle fahren die Linien elf und vierundzwanzig.
Tourist	**Entschuldigen Sie bitte,** wie komme ich **zum Bahnhof?**
Passer-by	Sie steigen in die Straßenbahnlinien zehn, zwölf oder vierzehn und fahren drei Stationen weit. Dann sind Sie in fünf Minuten dort.

wie komme ich . . . ? *how do I get . . . ?*
dann sind Sie in fünf Minuten dort *then you'll be there in five minutes*

Announcements in the tram or underground

'Nächste Haltestelle Theaterplatz. Sie haben Umsteigemöglichkeiten in Richtung Hoechst mit den Linien 10 und 12, in Richtung Zoo mit der Linie 23, in Richtung Heerstraße mit der Linie 19.'

'Nächste Haltestelle Hauptbahnhof. Fahrtende. Bitte aussteigen.'

'Nächste Haltestelle Hügelstraße. Sie haben Umsteigemöglichkeiten in Richtung Zoo mit der Linie 15, in Richtung Neu-Isenburg mit der Linie 27.'

'Nächste Haltestelle Weser-Münchenerstraße.

Nächste Haltestelle Theaterplatz. Sie haben Umsteigemöglichkeiten in Richtung Enkheim mit der Linie 18.

Nächste Haltestelle Zoologischer Garten. Fahrtende.
Bitte aussteigen.'

bitte aussteigen! *all change please!*
Sie haben Umsteigemöglichkeiten in Richtung *there are
connections to . . .*

Travelling by train

Tourist	Wann fährt **der nächste Zug nach Braunschweig, bitte?**
Official	Braunschweig? 16.55. Gleis 7.
Tourist	Wann fährt **der nächste Zug nach Minden, bitte?**
Official	16.55. Gleis 14.
Tourist	Wann fährt **der nächste Zug nach Celle?**
Official	Um 17 Uhr.
Tourist	Wann fährt **der nächste Zug nach Würzburg, bitte?**
Official	Nach Würzburg? 17.27.
Tourist	Wann fährt **der nächste Zug nach Kassel, bitte?**
Official	17.31, auf Gleis 3.

Beginning of side two, cassette two

Tourist	**Wann kommt der Zug** in Göttingen **an?**
Official	Um 11.16 Uhr.
Tourist	**Wann kommt der Zug** in Köln **an?**
Official	Um 18.38 Uhr.

wann fährt der nächste Zug nach . . . ? *when does the next train
leave for . . . ?*
auf Gleis zehn *platform ten*
wann kommt der Zug in . . . an? *when does the train arrive in . . . ?*

Language summary

● WHAT YOU NEED TO SAY

Telling the taxi driver where to take you

Bahnhof, bitte
Flughafen, bitte
Hotel Erlkönig, bitte
Theater, bitte

Asking for information

Entschuldigen Sie . . .
Entschuldigen Sie, ein Hotel, bitte?
Ein Taxistand, bitte?
Eine Tankstelle, bitte?
Die Haltestelle, bitte?
Die nächste Bushaltestelle?

Paying the fare and tipping

Was macht das?
Stimmt so

Enquiring about trains

Der nächste Zug nach Würzburg?
Wann kommt der Zug an?

● WHAT YOU NEED TO LISTEN OUT FOR

Public announcements

Zug nach Köln
Abfahrt sieben Uhr neunzehn
Ankunft dreizehn Uhr fünf
Gleis sieben
Nächste Haltestelle
Linie 5
in Richtung
Umsteigemöglichkeiten
Fahrtende
Bitte aussteigen! *get out, please*

Explanations

When referring to public transport, times are given by the 24-hour clock, e.g. **siebzehn Uhr zwanzig** (= 5.20 p.m.). Otherwise you'll hear **acht Uhr, zehn Minuten vor neun** (8.50), **zwanzig Minuten nach elf** (11.20). But take care!: half-past the hour is expressed quite differently from English — **halb drei** means *half-way to three,* i.e. 2.30.

Exercises

1 On three tram journeys you hear these announcements. How do you get to your destination each time? Answer in English.

You want to go to the zoo:
'Nächste Haltestelle Theaterplatz. Sie haben Umsteigemöglichkeiten in Richtung Eckenheim mit der Linie vierzehn, in Richtung Zoo mit der Linie dreiundzwanzig.'

You want to go to the theatre:
'Nächste Haltestelle Hügelstraße. Sie haben Umsteigemöglichkeiten in Richtung Theaterplatz mit der Linie fünfzehn.'

You want to get to the main railway station:
'Nächste Haltestelle Hauptbahnhof. Fahrtende. Bitte aussteigen.'

2 You're at the station and want to go to Friedrichshafen. You hear this announcement:

'Schnellzug nach Friedrichshafen. Abfahrt elf Uhr sechs, Ankunft fünfzehn Uhr zehn. Gleis zwölf.'

Which platform do you go to?.................................
When does the train leave?.................................
When does it arrive?.................................

This time you want to go to Frankfurt. This is the announcement you hear:

'Intercityzug nach Frankfurt, Abfahrt Gleis acht, neunzehn Uhr zehn, Ankunft dreiundzwanzig Uhr einunddreißig.'

Which platform do you go to?...........................

When does the train leave?...........................

When does it arrive?...........................

3 You've a plane to catch:

Ask the hotel receptionist to get you a taxi...........................
....

Tell the taxi driver where to take you...........................
....

Ask him what the fare is...........................
...........................?

You can't understand. *What* did he say?...........................
...........................?

In desperation you look at the meter: it says 24.50 DM.

How much do you give him?...........................

How do you tell him to keep the change?...........................
....

4 You want to go to the city centre. Stop someone and ask politely:

where the nearest bus-stop is...........................?

where the underground is...........................?

where the taxi rank is...........................?

This time you're at the station on your way to Darmstadt. Find out:

when the next train leaves...........................?

what time it arrives...........................?

5 What are you being advised to do? Choose from the three alternatives.

Aussteigen, bitte	a	Get in the tram
	b	Get off the tram
	c	Get out of the way

Knopf drücken	a	Press the button
	b	Mind your head
	c	Get off the bus

Fahren Sie mit der U-Bahn	a	Take the bus
	b	Take the tram
	c	Take the underground

Am besten nehmen Sie den Bus	a	Get on the train
	b	Get off the bus
	c	Go by bus

It's worth knowing

Taking a taxi

To get a taxi you usually have to telephone the taxi centre (**Taxizentrale**) or find a taxi rank (**Taxistand**). Hailing a taxi on the move rarely works. You tip the driver as you would the waiter by rounding up the amount.

Travelling by public transport

When you go by bus, tram or underground you're usually expected to buy your ticket before you board. This you can do at the automatic machines at the stops. In many towns and cities you're not allowed to get on without a ticket. For long distance journeys on the famous yellow Swiss Postal Coaches you can book your seat at post offices.

Some signs and public notices

ABFAHRT	*departure*
ANKUNFT	*arrival*
AUSKUNFT	*information*
AUSGANG	*exit*
EINGANG	*entrance*
KEIN EINGANG	*no entry*
FAHRKARTEN	*tickets*
OFFEN	*open*
GESCHLOSSEN	*closed*
DRÜCKEN	*push*
KNOPF DRÜCKEN	*press the button*
ZIEHEN	*pull*
GEFAHR	*danger*
DAMEN	*ladies*
HERREN	*gentlemen*

Bushaltestelle *bus stop*

Information *information*

Straßenbahnhaltestelle *tram stop*

Apotheke *chemist*

arrival   *departure*

5 Getting the essentials

Conversations

Finding out where places are . . . if you're on foot

Tourist **Wo ist** hier **die Post?**
Passer-by Die Post? Hier die Straße 'runter, dann rechts um die Ecke, dann kommen Sie ans Postamt.

hier die Straße 'runter *down this street*
rechts um die Ecke *right at the corner*

Tourist **Bitte, wo ist die Bushaltestelle?**
Passer-by Die nächste Straße links und dann noch ungefähr zweihundert Meter, und dann sehen Sie die Bushaltestelle schon.

die nächste Straße links *the next street on the left*
noch ungefähr zweihundert Meter *about another 200 metres*

Tourist **Entschuldigen Sie bitte, wo ist die nächste Straßenbahnhaltestelle** hier?
Passer-by Sie gehen erstmal geradeaus und dann nach rechts, und ungefähr nach zweihundert Metern kommen Sie zu der Haltestelle.

Sie gehen erstmal geradeaus *first go straight on*

Guest **Wo ist das Restaurant, bitte?**
Receptionist Bitte hier geradeaus.

Tourist Wann fährt **der nächste Zug nach Minden?**
Clerk Neun Uhr vierundvierzig.
Tourist Und von welchem **Gleis?**

Clerk	Gleis vierzehn.
Tourist	**Wo ist das, bitte?**
Clerk	Auf der rechten Seite gegenüber.

auf der rechten Seite gegenüber *on the right-hand side opposite*

| Jürgen | **Hotel Falkenstein, wo ist das, bitte?** |
| Passer-by | Das Hotel Falkenstein? Das kann ich Ihnen leider nicht sagen. Tut mir leid. |

das kann ich Ihnen leider nicht sagen *I'm afraid I can't tell you*
tut mir leid *sorry*

Jürgen	**Entschuldigen Sie. Hotel Falkenstein, wo ist das, bitte?**
Passer-by	Gleich hier um die nächste Ecke . . .
2nd Passer-by	Gleich hier links um die Ecke.

um die nächste Ecke *round the next corner*
gleich hier links *immediately to the left here*

. . . if you're driving

Passer-by	Da fahren Sie jetzt am besten die nächste Straße rechts . . .
Motorist	**Ja,** rechts.
Passer-by	. . . und dann die zweite Straße wieder rechts, und dann kommen Sie auf so eine große Straße, und da fahren Sie wieder rechts. Und dann ist das auch schon beschildert.

da fahren Sie die nächste Straße links *take the next street on the left*
am besten *the best thing is*
dann ist das beschildert *then it's signposted*

At the bank

Bank clerk	Wenn Sie hier unten bitte unterschreiben wollen.
Tourist	**Ja.**
Bank clerk	Danke. Und jetzt das ist eine Nummer für Sie. Mit dieser Nummer

gehen Sie bitte zur Kasse. Die ist
genau gegenüber.

hier unten *down here*
wenn Sie unterschreiben wollen *if you would please sign*
zur Kasse *to the cash desk*
genau gegenüber *directly opposite*

Bank clerk	Gehen Sie zur Kasse. Das ist Ihre Nummer.
Customer	**Wo ist die Kasse?**
Bank clerk	Hier geradeaus.
Customer	**Wo ist die Kasse, bitte?**
Bank clerk	Die Kasse ist gleich hier links nebenan.

gleich hier links nebenan *just next door here on the left*

Language summary

● WHAT YOU NEED TO SAY

Finding out where places are
Wo ist das Restaurant?
Wo ist das, bitte?

● WHAT YOU NEED TO LISTEN OUT FOR

Being given directions	**When someone can't help you**
geradeaus	Das kann ich Ihnen nicht sagen
gleich links	Tut mir leid
nach 200 Metern	
die erste Straße rechts	
die zweite Straße links	
die nächste Straße links	
die nächste Straße rechts	
auf der rechten Seite	
um die Ecke	
gegenüber	

Explanations

Notice how numbers change when you say first, second, etc.

die **erste** Straße	*first*
die **zweite** Straße	*second*
die **dritte** Straße	*third*
die **vierte** Straße	*fourth*
die **fünfte** Straße	*fifth*

You'll probably have noticed throughout this course that the endings on some words vary according to the context:

die erst**e** Straße links	auf der recht**en** Seite
ein groß**es** Bier	der nächst**e** Zug nach Minden

This is because some words have different endings according to how they are used in the sentence. At this stage there's no need to worry about this. You'll be understood even if you make mistakes and when you're talking to other people the main thing, after all, is to be able to pick out the essential meaning of what they say.

Exercises

1 You've asked people for directions. What are they telling you to do? Choose from the three alternatives.

Nehmen Sie die zweite Straße links

  a Take the first on the left
  b Take the second on the left
  c Take the second on the right

Gehen Sie hier geradeaus

  a Go straight on
  b Go immediately right
  c Take a bus

Nehmen Sie die nächste Straße rechts	a Take the first on the left
	b Take the second street to the right
	c Take the next street on the right
Gehen Sie um die nächste Ecke	a Go round the next corner
	b Cross the road
	c Go straight on
Gehen Sie gleich links	a Turn immediately right
	b Turn immediately left
	c Go straight on
Gegenüber, auf der rechten Seite	a Opposite on the right
	b Straight ahead on the right
	c Take the second road on the right

2 Asking for places. What would you ask a passer-by — as simply as possible?

You have to catch a train but you don't know where the station is:..?

You've booked a room at the Hotel Waldsee but can't find the hotel:..?

You're looking for the post office:..............................?

You're in a hurry and want a taxi but you can't see a taxi rank:..?

You want to catch a bus but you don't know where the nearest stop is:..?

You need to cash some traveller's cheques and want to get to the nearest bank:..?

You're running short of petrol and want the nearest
petrol station:...?

3 You're at the spot marked X on the map.
You ask a passer-by for directions. Does he
show you the right way? **Ja oder nein?**

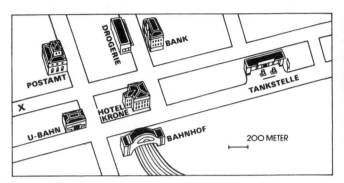

You want to go to the underground:
Hier die Straße 'runter, dann rechts um
die Ecke. ....

You want to go to the bank:
Ja, die zweite Straße links, und dann finden
Sie die Bank auf der linken Seite. ....

You want to go to the station:
Ja, die erste Straße rechts und dann links.
Der Bahnhof ist auf der rechten Seite. ....

You want to go to the Krone Hotel:
Sie gehen geradeaus, dann die zweite Straße
rechts, und dann liegt das Hotel Krone auf der
rechten Seite. ....

You want to go to the petrol station:
Fahren Sie geradeaus, dann die zweite Straße
rechts, dann links, und dann sehen Sie die
Tankstelle auf der rechten Seite. ....

You want to go to the chemist's:
Die zweite Straße rechts, dann liegt die Drogerie
nach zweihundert Metern auf der linken Seite.   ....

You want to go to the post office:
Ja, Sie gehen geradeaus und die erste Straße
links, und dann sehen Sie das Postamt.   ....

4 Asking for things. Again, how would you ask — as
simply as possible?

You're in a restaurant and want to see the menu:

....

In a café you decide to have a large beer:

....

You're in a **Drogerie** and need some toothpaste:

....

You want to know if a shop has postcards:

.... ?

You've bought three cards. Now you need stamps for
them: ....

In a **Konditorei** you order cups of coffee for yourself
and your friend: ....

You've run out of cigarettes. Perhaps the café
sells English ones? .... ?

You've finished your meal and want to pay the bill:

.... !

You're in your hotel room and order breakfast by
phone: ....

....

5 When you've read this conversation, try to work out the answers to the questions below—in English. Look up any words you need in the word list at the end of the book.

Receptionist	Guten Abend! Bitte, was wünschen Sie?
Guest	Guten Abend! Für mich ist ein Zimmer reserviert.
Receptionist	Ja. Ihr Name, bitte?
Guest	Frank.
Receptionist	Einen Moment, bitte . . . Ja, Sie haben Zimmer Nummer zwei im ersten Stock. Wo ist Ihr Gepäck?
Guest	Das Gepäck ist im Taxi. Hat das Zimmer Dusche?
Receptionist	Ja, es hat Dusche. Es hat Dusche und WC.
Guest	Ah gut. Was kostet das Zimmer?
Receptionist	Fünfzig Mark mit Frühstück.
Guest	Was gibt es zum Frühstück?
Receptionist	Wir servieren Kaffee, Brötchen, Butter, Gelée, Käse oder Wurst, ein Ei und Orangensaft.
Guest	Gut. Wann gibt es Frühstück?
Receptionist	Von sieben bis zehn Uhr.
Guest	Hat das Zimmer Telefon?
Receptionist	Leider nicht.

Has the guest already reserved a room at the hotel?

....

What is the guest's name?..............................

Which room is he to have?..............................

Where has he left his luggage?.........................

Does the room have a shower?.........................

What else does it have?..................................

Is there a phone in the room?..........................

How much does the room cost?........................

Does the price include breakfast?.....................

What does the breakfast consist of?...................................

....

When can you have breakfast?...

6 You've asked the way to the city centre and are given the answer below. Pick out and underline the absolute minimum of information **you** need to get there. Mark the route on the map.

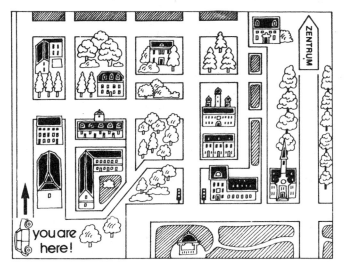

'Fahren Sie die erste Straße rechts, diese Straße bis zum Ende, wieder rechts, wieder bis zum Ende, dann kommen Sie an eine Ampel, dort biegen Sie nach links ab. Fahren Sie geradeaus weiter, bis Sie an eine große Kreuzung kommen. Dort biegen Sie links ab. Sie fahren ungefähr zwei Kilometer weiter und sind dann direkt im Zentrum. Gute Fahrt!'

die Kreuzung *crossroads*

It's worth knowing

Travelling by car

In all German-speaking countries the rule is, of course, drive on the right. Traffic regulations are similar to those in the U.S. In built-up areas in Germany and Austria the speed limit is 50 kilometres per hour (in Switzerland it's 60 kph). Elsewhere, except on motorways, the limit is 100 kph. Parking restrictions are by and large the same as in the U.S., and you'll find the familiar parking meter, too! Where parking is permitted many towns insist on the use of a parking disc, which you can get from garages, tourist offices, tobacconists, and so on. One point worth bearing in mind: policemen are empowered to fine you on the spot for breaking traffic rules—speeding, for example. Your motoring organisation in the U.S. should provide you with details of the traffic regulations of the country you intend to visit.

If you're driving, look out for these signs:

Einbahnstraße
one-way street

Vorsicht!
careful!

werktags
weekdays
9-12 h

Parkverbot *no parking*

Keine Einfahrt
no entry

Vorfahrtsrecht
Your right of way

Gegenverkehr
two-way traffic

Anfang der
Autobahn
*beginning of
motorway*

Ausfahrt
exit (on motorways)

Ende der
Autobahn
*End of
motorway*

Umleitung

Umleitung
diversion

Changing money

Banking hours vary a little according to the bank but
generally banks are open from eight or nine in the
morning until four in the afternoon. They are all
closed on Saturdays, except in major resorts where
some banks do open on Saturday mornings in
summer. Most banks display their opening hours at
the entrance and sometimes the current rates of
exchange, too. It's always best to change your cash
or cheques at the bank as exchange bureaux, such as
you see at frontier crossing points or in some shops,
nearly always give slightly less than the official rate.
When you change your money in hotels or
restaurants, as sometimes you can, you'll usually be
charged a 'commission'. You can often change
money outside banking hours at main railway
stations and airports.

Can you 'GET BY'?

For notes on working through these tests see page 8. The answers are on page 67.

Test 1 Getting food and drink

---

1 One afternoon you meet Herr Schmidt. What do you say?

a Guten Abend, Herr Schmidt.
b Guten Morgen, Herr Schmidt.
c Guten Tag, Herr Schmidt.

2 In a café, Herr Schmidt offers you a beer, which you don't fancy. What do you say?

a Bitte schön.
b Nein, danke.
c Nein, ein kleines Bier, bitte.

3 He asks what you'd like. You tell him tea with lemon. What do you say?

a Tee mit Zitrone, bitte.
b Nehmen Sie mit Zitrone oder Sahne?
c Tee, bitte.

4 He then asks you: **Möchten Sie Obstkuchen?** Is he asking:

a if you want to leave?
b if you want some fruit?
c if you want some fruit tart?

5 When the waiter comes, Herr Schmidt orders your tea and for himself **ein Kännchen Kaffee und Obstkuchen mit Sahne.** What is he having?

a A pot of coffee and fruit tart with cream.
b A pot of tea with cream cake.
c A large beer with fruit tart.

6 You're in a café with a friend. You want the waitress and call her saying:........................!

7 You ask for two cups of coffee:..................

....

8 You also want two pieces of fruit tart: ....

....

9 You offer your friend a cigarette, saying: ....

....

10 Later you ask for the bill: .... !

Test 2   Getting your shopping done

1 You're in a shop and hear the assistant say:
Haben Sie sonst noch einen Wunsch? Is she asking:
a   if you want a carrier bag?
b   if you want anything else?
c   if you have a watch?

2 You ask for toothpaste, saying:
a   Zahnkrem, bitte.
b   Puder, bitte.
c   Eine Tüte, bitte.

3 She tells you that your purchases cost **sechs Mark achtundneunzig.** You give her:
a   6,98 DM
b   6,89 DM
c   8,98 DM

4 In the post office you want to know how much it costs to send a letter to England. You ask:
a   Was kostet eine Postkarte nach England, bitte?
b   Was kosten die englischen Briefmarken, bitte?
c   Was kostet ein Brief nach England, bitte?

5 You want three stamps at 80 and four at 70.
You say:
a   Drei Briefmarken zu achtzehn und vier zu siebzehn, bitte.
b   Drei Briefmarken zu achtzig und vier zu siebzig, bitte.

c Vier Briefmarken zu achtzig und drei zu siebzig, bitte.

How would you:

6 ask how much a bottle of wine costs? . . . . ?

7 ask a petrol pump attendant to fill up your tank? . . . .

8 ask if a shopkeeper has English cigarettes? . . . . ?

9 ask for a small packet of plaster? . . . .

10 ask for a bag to carry your shopping? . . . .

Test 3 Getting a hotel room

1 When you arrive at a hotel the receptionist tells you: **Wir haben kein Zimmer mehr frei.** She means:

a they haven't any rooms left.
b they only have one room free.
c they have kept a room free for you.

2 You find a hotel and ask the price of a room with a shower. You say:

a Was kostet ein Zimmer mit Bad, bitte?
b Was kostet ein Zimmer mit Dusche, bitte?
c Ein Doppelzimmer ohne Dusche, bitte.

3 You tell the receptionist you want a double room with shower. You say:

a Ich möchte ein Einzelzimmer mit Dusche, bitte.
b Ich möchte ein Doppelzimmer ohne Dusche, bitte.
c Ich möchte ein Doppelzimmer mit Dusche, bitte.

4 You'd like a single room for two nights. You say:

a Ein Einzelzimmer für drei Nächte, bitte.
b Ein Einzelzimmer für zwei Nächte, bitte.
c Ein Doppelzimmer für Nächte, bitte.

5 You ask if the price includes breakfast, saying:

a Ist das mit Frühstück?

b Frühstück, bitte.

c Was kostet ein normales, deutsches Frühstück, bitte?

6 The receptionist at the hotel asks you: **Und wie lange bleiben Sie?** She wants to know:.............

....

7 You and your wife/husband want a double room for three nights. You say: ....

....

8 Ask for your key at reception. Your room number is 36...

9 In your hotel room you order breakfast by phone saying: ....

10 You also want an egg. You say: ....

Test 4   Getting about

1 You've asked a passer-by how to get to the station. He tells you: **Wenn Sie zum Bahnhof wollen, fahren Sie am besten mit der U-Bahn.** Is he saying:

a he's sorry, he doesn't know the way?

b that it's best to take the underground?

c the best way to get there is by tram?

2 You want to know when the next train goes to Cologne. You say:

a Wann fährt der nächste Zug nach Köln, bitte?

b Wann kommt der Zug in Köln an, bitte?

c Schnellzug nach Köln, Abfahrt Gleis acht.

3 The official says: **Zwanzig Uhr zehn, Gleis neun.** What is he telling you?

a That your train leaves at twenty past ten from platform nine.

b That your train leaves at ten to eight from platform nineteen.

c That your train leaves at ten past eight from platform nine.

4 You want to know when your train gets into Göttingen. You ask the ticket collector:

a Wann kommt der Zug in Göttingen an, bitte?

b Wann fährt der Zug nach Göttingen ab, bitte?

c Wann fährt der nächste Zug nach Göttingen, bitte?

5 You get into a taxi and tell the driver to take you to the airport. You say:

a Bahnhof, bitte.

b Marktplatz, bitte.

c Flughafen, bitte.

6 You want to catch the bus. Ask where the nearest bus-stop is: ....?

7 Ask someone which bus goes to Koblenz:

....?

8 Ask your taxi-driver how much you owe him:

....?

9 Ask when the next train goes to Bonn: ....
....?

10 Listening to the station announcer, you hear that your train leaves at **siebzehn Uhr fünfundzwanzig**. When is that? ....

Test 5 Getting the essentials

1 You want to know where the underground train goes from. You ask:

a Fahren Sie mit der U-Bahn?

b Wo fährt die U-Bahn ab, bitte?

c Wo ist die Bushaltestelle, bitte?

2 Asking for the post-office, you say:

a Bitte, wo ist die Post?

b Haben Sie Postkarten, bitte?

c Wo ist das Hotel zur Post, bitte?

3 Asking directions in the street, you're told:
Nehmen Sie die dritte Straße rechts.
What do you do?

a Turn immediately right.

b Take the first street on the right.

c Take the third street on the right.

4 You've asked someone for directions to the station. He says: **Das kann ich Ihnen leider nicht sagen.** What is he saying?

a He's sorry, he can't say.

b He's asking you to repeat your question.

c He's telling you you're heading in the wrong direction.

5 You stop someone to ask where the nearest tram-stop is. You say:

a Entschuldigen Sie bitte, wo fährt die U-Bahn ab?

b Entschuldigen Sie, wo ist hier die nächste Straßenbahnhaltestelle, bitte?

c Entschuldigen Sie, wo ist die nächste Bushaltestelle, bitte?

6 You ask the porter the way to your platform. He replies **gleich links.** Which way do you go? . . . .

. . . .

7 Trying to find your hotel, you're told it's **rechts um die Ecke.** Where do you go? . . . .

. . . .

8 Ask where the bus-stop is: . . . . ?

9 In your hotel, ask where the restaurant is: . . . .

. . . . ?

10 You want to change money. Ask where the nearest bank is: . . . . ?

Reference section

Pronunciation guide

You pronounce German words exactly as they are written. Practically every letter is pronounced.

German vowel sounds are "pure" and do not glide into a second vowel sound as is the case in American English ("day" as "day-ee" or "boat" as "bow-oot"). Vowel combinations in German are spelled with two letters, as shown.

Vowels are long when doubled **(Tee)**, before 'h' **(gehen)** and usually before a single consonant **(gut)**. They are short before double consonants **(Herr)**. An *Umlaut* (shown by two dots over the vowel) indicates a change in pronunciation.

Sounds that differ radically from English are given below. The English equivalents are only an approximation.

a	(long)	as 'a' in 'father'	Sahne
a	(short)	as 'o' in 'top'	Tasse, danke
ä	(long)	as 'a' in 'late'	Käse
ä	(short)	as 'e' in 'set'	Kännchen
au		as 'ow' in 'how'	Frau, auch
äu		as 'oi' in 'oil'	Fräulein
ch	(hard)	as 'ch' in Scottish 'loch' after a, o, u, au	macht, noch, Kuchen, auch
ch	(soft)	as whispered 'h' in 'huge'	nicht, rechts
chs		as 'x'	sechs
e	(long)	as first part of 'a' in 'gate'	Tee
e	(short)	as 'e' in 'set'	rechts
ei		as 'i' in 'nine'	nein, zwei
eu		as 'oi' in 'oil'	neun, deutsch
g		at the end of a word as -*ich*	Pfennig, zwanzig
i	(long)	as 'ee' in 'fee'	Ihr
i	(short)	as 'i' in 'sit'	bitte

ie		as 'ee' in 'fee'	Sie, Bier
		as 'ye' in 'yes' in some words of foreign origin	Linie
j		as 'y' in 'yes'	ja
o	(long)	as 'o' in 'home'	ohne, Ober
o	(short)	as 'o' in 'off'	kostet
ö	(long)	pout your lips and without moving them say 'a' as in 'day'	schön
ö	(short)	pout your lips and without moving them say 'e' as in 'pen'	möchten
sch		as 'sh'	Flasche
sp		as 'shp' at the beginning of a word	sprechen
st		as 'sht' at the beginning of a word	Stück, Straße
tz		as 'ts' in 'cats'	Platz
u	(long)	as 'oo' in 'moon'	Uhr, gut
u	(short)	as 'u' in 'full'	und, Bus
ü	(long)	pout your lips and without moving them say 'ee'	für, Tüte
ü	(short)	pout your lips and without moving them say short 'i'	fünf, Stück
v		as 'f'	voll
w		as 'v'	Wiedersehen, was
z		as 'ts' in 'cats'	zwei, Zimmer
ß		This letter is equivalent to 'ss'. It is used at the end of a word (Faß), before a consonant (bißchen) and after a long vowel (Straße) or vowel combination (dreißig).	

Numbers

0	null	10	zehn	20	zwanzig
1	eins	11	elf	21	einundzwanzig
2	zwei	12	zwölf	22	zweiundzwanzig
3	drei	13	dreizehn	23	dreiundzwanzig
4	vier	14	vierzehn	24	vierundzwanzig
5	fünf	15	fünfzehn	25	fünfundzwanzig
6	sechs	16	sechzehn	26	sechsundzwanzig
7	sieben	17	siebzehn	27	siebenundzwanzig
8	acht	18	achtzehn	28	achtundzwanzig
9	neun	19	neunzehn	29	neunundzwanzig

30	dreißig	80	achtzig
40	vierzig	90	neunzig
50	fünfzig	100	hundert
60	sechzig	200	zweihundert
70	siebzig	1000	tausend

Prices and times

These are usually written as follows:

Prices	35 DM	fünfunddreißig Mark
	2,58 DM	zwei Mark achtundfünfzig
Times	11.16 Uhr	elf Uhr sechzehn
	18.38 Uhr	achtzehn Uhr achtunddreißig

Days of the week

Sonntag	*Sunday*	Donnerstag	*Thursday*
Montag	*Monday*	Freitag	*Friday*
Dienstag	*Tuesday*	Samstag *or*	*Saturday*
Mittwoch	*Wednesday*	Sonnabend	

Months of the year

Januar	*January*	Juli	*July*
Februar	*February*	August	*August*
März	*March*	September	*September*
April	*April*	Oktober	*October*
Mai	*May*	November	*November*
Juni	*June*	Dezember	*December*

Answers to exercises

Programme 1

1 Guten Tag!; nein, danke; ein Glas Wein; zwei Tassen Kaffee; nein, danke.

2 Fräulein!; eine Tasse Kaffee, bitte; mit Sahne; noch ein Kaffee; Fräulein, bitte zahlen!

3 Herr Ober!; ein Bier, bitte; noch ein Bier, bitte; eine Tasse Kaffee und ein Glas Wein, bitte; eine Tasse Kaffee, ein Kännchen Tee und eine Flasche Wein, bitte; Herr Ober, zahlen bitte!; nein—zwei Bier, zwei Tassen Kaffee, ein Glas Wein, ein Kännchen Tee und eine Flasche Wein.

4 zehn Tassen Kaffee; acht Glas Wein; sechs Bier; sechs Tee.

5 b; a; c.

Programme 2

1 zu zwei fünfzig; (eine kleine Flasche) zu fünf Mark dreißig; (die Postkarten) zu fünfzig; eine kleine (Packung); fünf; eine Tasse; ein Stück; Normal.

2 a; b; c.

3 Was macht das?; die da; was kostet die?; eine Flasche Wein, bitte; was kostet eine Flasche?; zwei Flaschen Wein, bitte.

4 Guten Tag! Seife, bitte; Die Seife zu achtzig, bitte; Ja, eine Zahnbürste, bitte; Ja, bitte. Was kostet die?; Ja, Zahnkrem, bitte; Die kleine Packung; Nein, danke. Was macht das?; Ja, bitte.

5 Postcards 1.00 DM; stamps 1.00 DM; cigarettes 2.70 DM; matches 0.70 DM; plaster 1.20 DM; powder 1.10 DM; toothpaste 2.95 DM; total: zehn Mark sechsundfünfzig.

6 Dreiundzwanzig Mark und fünf Pfennig.

Programme 3

1 Cosmos; Falkenstein.

2 Ein Einzelzimmer für eine Nacht; ist das mit Frühstück?; ein Doppelzimmer mit Dusche, bitte; Tee mit Zitrone, bitte.

3 Guten Abend! Ein Zimmer, bitte; Nein, ein Doppelzimmer, bitte; Mit Bad; Was kostet das Zimmer?; Mit Frühstück?; Ja, bitte; Mein Name ist . . .; Wie bitte?; Ja, für eine Nacht.

Programme 4

1 To get to the zoo: leave the tram at the *Theaterplatz* and change to route 23. To get to the theatre: get off at *Hügelstraße* and take route 15. To get to the railway station: get off at the next stop.

2 For Friedrichshafen: platform 12 at 11.06, arriving 15.10. For Frankfurt: platform 8 at 19.10, arriving 23.31.

3 Ein Taxi, bitte; Flughafen, bitte; was macht das?; wie bitte?; 25 marks; (es) stimmt so.

4 (Entschuldigen Sie,) die nächste Bushaltestelle, bitte?; (entschuldigen Sie,) die U-Bahn, bitte?; (entschuldigen Sie,) ein Taxistand, bitte?; (wann fährt) der nächste Zug nach Darmstadt?; wann kommt der Zug in Darmstadt an?

5 b; a; c; c.

Programme 5

1 b; a; c; a; b; a.

2 Der Bahnhof, bitte?; das Hotel Waldsee, bitte?; die Post, bitte; ein Taxistand, bitte?; die nächste Bushaltestelle, bitte?; die nächste Bank, bitte?; die nächste Tankstelle, bitte?

3 Ja; nein — die zweite Straße links, und dann finden Sie die Bank auf der *rechten* Seite; ja; ja; nein — fahren Sie geradeaus, dann die zweite Straße rechts, dann links, und dann sehen Sie die Tankstelle auf der *linken* Seite; nein — die zweite Straße *links*, dann liegt die Drogerie nach zweihundert Metern auf der linken Seite; ja.

4 Die (Speise) Karte, bitte; ein großes Bier, bitte; Zahnkrem, bitte; Postkarten, bitte?; drei Briefmarken, bitte; zwei Tassen Kaffee, bitte; englische Zigaretten, bitte?; zahlen, bitte!; Frühstück, bitte.

5 Yes; Frank; Room 2 on the first floor; in the taxi; yes; WC; no; 50 marks; yes; coffee, rolls, butter and jam, cheese or sliced sausage, an egg and orange juice; from 7-10 am.

6 erste Straße rechts; bis zum Ende; rechts; bis zum Ende; links; Kreuzung; links; zwei Kilometer weiter.

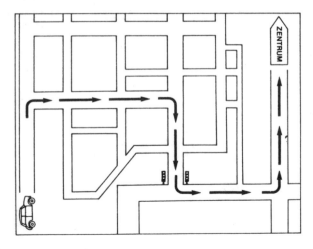

Answers to Can you 'GET BY'?

Test 1   1 c. 2 b. 3 a. 4 c. 5 a. 6 Fräulein! 7 Zwei Tassen Kaffee, bitte. 8 Und zwei Stück Obstkuchen. 9 Eine Zigarette? 10 Zahlen, bitte!

Test 2   1 b. 2 a. 3 a. 4 c. 5 b. 6 Was kostet eine Flasche Wein? 7 Voll, bitte. 8 Haben Sie englische Zigaretten? 9 Eine kleine Packung Pflaster, bitte. 10 Eine Tüte, bitte.

Test 3   1 a. 2 b. 3 c. 4 b. 5 a. 6 How long you're staying. 7 Ein Doppelzimmer für drei Nächte, bitte. 8 Mein Schlüssel, bitte. Zimmer Nummer sechsunddreißig. 9 Frühstück, bitte. 10 Ein Ei, bitte.

Test 4   1 b. 2 a. 3 c. 4 a. 5 c. 6 Die nächste Bushaltestelle, bitte? 7 Welcher Bus fährt nach Koblenz, bitte? 8 Was macht das? 9 Wann fährt der nächste Zug nach Bonn? 10 5.25 pm.

Test 5   1 b. 2 a. 3 c. 4 a. 5 b. 6 Left. 7 Right, round the corner. 8 Wo ist die Bushaltestelle, bitte? 9 Wo ist das Restaurant, bitte? 10 Wo ist die nächste Bank, bitte?

German–English word list

Plural forms of nouns are given in brackets.
The English meanings apply to the words as they are used in *Getting by in German*.

A

der Abend (-e) *evening;* guten Abend! *good evening*
die Abfahrt (-en) *departure*
achtzig *eighty*
alles *everything*
am besten *best*
die Ampel (-n) *traffic lights*
die Ankunft (̈e) *arrival*
ans *to the*
der Apfelstrudel *kind of apple turnover*
die Apotheke (-n) *chemist's*
auch *also*
auf *on;* auf Wiedersehen! *goodbye*
ausgebucht *fully booked*
aussteigen *to get out*

B

das Bad (̈er) *bath*
der Bahnhof (̈e) *station*
die Bank (-en) *bank*
beschildert *signposted*
besetzt *engaged, full*
besten: am besten *best*
biegen Sie . . . ab *you turn*
der Bienenstich *kind of honey and almond cake*
das Bier (-e) *beer*
bis *till;* bis zum/zur *as far as*
bißchen: ein bißchen *a little, bit*
bitte, bitte schön *please, not at all, here you are;* bitte schön? *yes please?*
bleiben *to stay*
Braunschweig *Brunswick*
der Brief (-e) *letter*
die Briefmarke (-n) *stamp*
bringen *to bring*

das Brot (-e) *bread*
das Brötchen (-) *bread roll*
der Bus (-se) *bus*
die Butter *butter*

D

da *there*
die Dame (-n) *lady;* Damen *ladies (toilets)*
Dank: schönen Dank! *thank you very much*
danke *thank you;* danke schön *thank you very much;* danke vielmals! *many thanks*
dann *then*
das *the, that*
dazu *with it*
den *the*
der *the*
deutsch, deutsches *German*
die *the, that one, those*
diese, dieser *this*
direkt *directly*
DM = Deutschmark *German mark (unit of currency)*
das Doppelzimmer (-) *double room*
dort *there*
drei *three*
dreißig *thirty*
dreiundzwanzig *twenty-three*
dritte *third*
die Drogerie (-n) *chemist's*
drücken *to press*
die Dusche (-n) *shower*

E

die Ecke (-n) *corner*
das Ei (-er) *egg*
ein, eine, einen *a, one*

eins *one*

das Einzelzimmer (-) *single room*

das Ende (-n) *end*

England *England*

englische, englischen *English*

entschuldigen Sie *excuse me*

erste, ersten *first*

erstmal *first of all*

es *it*

extra *extra*

F

fahren *to travel, go*

die Fahrkarte (-n) *ticket*

die Fahrt (-en) *journey*

fährt *goes*

fährt . . . ab *leaves*

das Fahrtende (-n) *terminus*

finden *to find*

der Finger (-) *finger*

die Flasche (-n) *bottle*

der Flughafen (⁻) *airport*

der Franken (-) *franc (Swiss unit of currency)*

die Frau (-en) *woman, wife;* Frau . . . *Mrs. . . .*

das Fräulein (-) *young lady;* Fräulein! *waitress!* Fräulein . . . *Miss . . .*

frei *free, available*

das Frühstück *breakfast*

frühstücken *to have breakfast*

fünf *five*

fünfte *fifth*

fünfundachtzig *eighty-five*

fünfzig *fifty*

für *for*

G

garni: ein Hotel garni *hotel serving breakfast only*

Garten: Zoologischer Garten *zoo*

das Gedeck (-e) *set meal*

gegenüber *opposite*

gehen *to go*

das Gelée (-s) *jam, jelly*

genau *directly*

das Gepäck *luggage*

geradeaus *straight on*

gern(e) *gladly*

geschlossen *closed*

gibt's = gibt es *there is*

das Glas (⁻er) *glass*

gleich *immediately*

das Gleis (-e) *platform, track*

der Groschen (-) *Austrian currency, 1/100 of a Schilling*

groß, große, großes *big, large*

gut, gute *good*

H

haben *to have*

halb *half*

die Haltestelle (-n) *stop*

hat *has*

hätten: was hätten Sie gerne? *what would you like?*

der Hauptbahnhof (⁻e) *main station*

der Herr (-en) *gentleman;* Herren *gents (toilets);* Herr Ober! *waiter!* Herr . . . *Mr. . . .*

hier *here*

das Hotel (-s) *hotel*

hundert *a hundred*

I

ich *I*

Ihnen *(to) you*

Ihr, Ihre *your*

im *at the, in the*

in *in*

der Intercityzug (⁻e) *Inter-City train*

ist *is*

J

ja *yes*
jawohl *yes, certainly*
jetzt *now*

K

der Kaffee *coffee*
kann: ich kann *I can*
das Kännchen (-) *small pot*
die Karte (-n) *menu, card, ticket*
der Käse (-) *cheese*
der Käsekuchen (-) *cheesecake*
die Kasse (-n) *cash desk*
kein *no, not any*
der *or* das Kilometer (-) *kilometre*
der Kiosk (-e) *kiosk*
die Klasse (-n) *class*
klein, kleine, kleines *small*
der Knopf (-̈e) *button*
Köln *Cologne*
kommen *to come, get to*
kommt . . . an *arrives*
die Konditorei (-en) *cake shop, café*
die Konfitüre (-n) *jam*
können *to be able*
kosten *to cost*
die Kreuzung (-en) *crossroads*
der Kuchen (-) *cake*

L

langsam *slowly*
leid: das tut mir leid *I'm sorry*
leider *unfortunately*
liegen *to lie, be situated*
die Linie (-n) *line, route*
linken: auf der linken Seite *on the left-hand side*
links *on or to the left*

M

macht: das macht *that makes, comes to;* was macht das? *how much does that come to?*

die Mark (-) *mark (German unit of currency)*
der Marktplatz (-̈e) *market place*
die Marmelade (-n) *jam*
mehr *more*
mein, meine *my*
das Menü (-s) *set meal*
der *or* das Meter (-) *metre*
mich *me*
die Minute (-n) *minute*
mit *with*
möchte: ich möchte *I'd like*
möchten Sie? *would you like?*
der Moment (-e) *moment;* im Moment *at the moment*
der Morgen (-) *morning;* guten Morgen! *good morning*
München *Munich*

N

nach *after, to*
nächste *next, nearest*
die Nacht (-̈e) *night*
der Name (-n) *name*
nebenan *next door*
nein *no*
neunzehn *nineteen*
nicht *not*
noch ein *another*
das Normal *economy-grade petrol*
normal, normales *normal*
die Nummer (-n) *number*

O

Ober: Herr Ober! *waiter!*
der Obstkuchen (-) *fruit tart*
oder *or*
offen *open*
ohne *without*
der Orangensaft *orange juice*

P

die Packung (-en) *packet*
der Paß (-̈sse) *passport*
die Person (-en) *person*

der Pfennig (-e) *pfennig (German currency, 1/100 of a mark)*

das Pflaster (-) *sticking plaster*

der Platz (-e) *square*

die Post *post, post office*

das Postamt (-er) *post office*

die Postkarte (-n) *postcard*

pro *per*

der Puder (-) *powder*

R

der Rappen (-) *centime (Swiss currency, 1/100 of a franc)*

rechten: auf der rechten Seite *on the right-hand side*

rechts *on or to the right*

reserviert *reserved*

das Restaurant (-s) *restaurant*

der Rheinwein (-e) *Rhine wine*

die Richtung (-en) *direction*

'runter *down*

S

sagen *to say, tell*

die Sahne *cream*

die Sahnetorte (-n) *cream gateau*

der Schilling (-e) *shilling (Austrian unit of currency)*

der Schlüssel (-) *key*

der Schnellzug (-e) *fast train*

die Schokolade (-n) *chocolate*

schon *already*

schön: danke schön, schönen Dank! *thank you very much*

das Schwarzbrot *coarse rye bread* (lit. *black bread*)

sechs *six*

sechzig *sixty*

sehen *to see*

sehr *very*

die Seife (-n) *soap*

die Seite (-n) *side*

die Selbstbedienung *self-service*

selbsttanken *to serve yourself petrol*

servieren *to serve*

Sie *you*

siebzig *seventy*

sind *are*

so *well then;* so eine *a kind of*

sonst noch (ein) *any other*

Spaß: viel Spaß! *have a good time! enjoy yourself!*

die Speisekarte (-n) *menu*

sprechen *to speak*

die Stadt (-e) *town*

die Stadtmitte *town centre*

die Station (-en) *stop*

steigen in *to get on*

stimmt (so) *that's alright, keep the change*

der Stock (-werke) *floor*

die Straße (-n) *street*

die Straßenbahn (-en) *tram*

das Streichholz (-er) *match*

das Stück (-e) *piece*

das Super *high-grade petrol*

T

der Tag (-e) *day;* guten Tag! lit. *good day!*

die Tankstelle (-n) *petrol station*

die Tasse (-n) *cup*

das Taxi (-s) *taxi*

der Taxistand (-e) *taxi rank*

der Tee *tea*

das Telefon (-e) *telephone*

das Theater (-) *theatre*

der Theaterplatz *Theatre Square*

die Toilette (-n) *toilet*

die Torte (-n) *tart, flan*

trinken *to drink*

tut: das tut mir leid *I'm sorry*

die Tüte (-n) *bag*

U

die U-Bahn *underground*
Uhr *o'clock*
um *at, round*
die Umsteigemöglichkeit (-en)
    connection (buses and
    trams)
und *and*
ungefähr *about*
unten: hier unten *down*
    here
unter *below*
unterschreiben *to sign*

V

verbinden *to connect, put*
    through
viel: viel Spaß! *have a good*
    time! enjoy yourself!
vielmals: danke vielmals!
    many thanks
voll *full*
volltanken *to fill up*
    (with petrol)
von *from*
vor *to*

W

wann? *when?*
was? *what?*
das WC *WC, toilet*
der Wein (-e) *wine*
weit *far*
weiter *further*
welcher? welchen? *which?*
wenn *if*

werktags *on working days*
wie? *how? what?*
wie bitte? *pardon?*
wie lange? *how long?*
wieder *again*
Wiedersehen! auf
    Wiedersehen! *goodbye*
wir *we*
wo? *where?*
der Wolf (-̈e) *wolf*
wollen *to want to*
wollen Sie? *would you?*
der Wunsch (-̈e) *wish*
wünschen *to wish, want*
die Wurst (-̈e) *sausage*

Z

zahlen *to pay*
die Zahnbürste (-n) *toothbrush*
die Zahnkrem *toothpaste*
das Zentrum (-tren) *town centre*
die Zigarette (-n) *cigarette*
das Zimmer (-) *room*
die Zitrone (-n) *lemon*
der Zoo (-s) *zoo*
zoologisch: Zoologischer
    Garten *zoo*
zu *to; at*
der Zug (-̈e) *train*
zum *to the;* zum Frühstück
    for breakfast
zur *to the*
zusammen *together*
zwanzig *twenty*
zwei *two*
zweite *second*
zwo = zwei

English–German word list

A

a, one *ein, eine, einen*
(to be) able *können* I can *ich kann;* can you? *können Sie?*
about *ungefähr*
adhesive tape *das Pflaster (-)*
after *nach*
again *wieder*
airport *der Flughafen (-)*
already *schon*
also *auch*
and *und*
another *noch ein*
any other *sonst noch ein/eine*
anything else? *sonst noch etwas?*
apple turnover *der Apfelstrudel*
arrival *die Ankunft (-e)*
arrives *kommt ... an*
as far as *bis zum/zur*
at *an/am/an der; in/im/in der; um* (with time expressions)
available *frei*

B

bag (sack) *die Tüte (-n)*
baggage *das Gepäck*
bank *die Bank (-en)*
bath *das Bad (-er)*
beer *das Bier (-e)*
below *unter*
best *am besten*
big *groß*
bit (a little) *ein bißchen*
booked up *ausgebucht*
bottle *die Flasche (-n)*
bread *das Brot (-e)*
bread roll *das Brötchen (-)*
(to have) breakfast *frühstücken*
breakfast *das Frühstück*
(to) bring *bringen*

Brunswick *Braunschweig*
bus *der Bus (-se)*
busy (telephone) *besetzt*
butter *die Butter*

C

cake *der Kuchen (-)*
card *die Karte (-n)*
cashier *die Kasse (-n)*
center (of town) *die Stadtmitte, das Zentrum*
change (keep ...) *stimmt so*
cheese *der Käse*
cheesecake *der Käsekuchen (-)*
chocolate *die Schokolade (-n)*
cigarette *die Zigarette (-n)*
city *die Stadt (-e)*
class *die Klasse (-n)*
closed *geschlossen*
coffee *der Kaffee*
(to) come *kommen*
(to) connect (telephone) *verbinden*
connection (bus, streetcar) *die Umsteigemöglichkeit (-en)*
corner *die Ecke (-n)*
(to) cost *kosten;* what does ... cost? *was kostet ...?*
cream *die Sahne*
cup *die Tasse (-n)*

D

day *der Tag;* hello *guten Tag!*
departure *die Abfahrt (-en)*
direction *die Richtung (-en)*
directly *direkt, genau*
down *'runter* (with verb of motion)
down here *hier unten*
down there *da unten*
drug store *die Drogerie (-n)*

E

egg *das Ei (-er)*
end *das Ende (-n)*
engaged (taxi) *besetzt*
evening *der Abend (-e);* good
  evening! *guten Abend!*
everything *alles*
excuse (me) *entschuldigen
  Sie!*

F

far *weit*
farther/further *weiter*
filling station *die Tankstelle
  (-n)*
(to) find *finden*
finger *der Finger (-)*
first *erste, ersten*
first of all *erstmal*
floor (storey) *der Stock (die
  Stockwerke)*
for *für;* is that for me? *ist
  das für mich?;* zu, zum,
  zur; what's for breakfast?
  was gibt es zum Frühstück?
  um; he asks for coffee.
  er bittet um Kaffee.
free *frei*
from *von*
full *besetzt (hotel)*
  voll (glass, gas tank, etc.)
fun *der Spaß;* have a good
  time! *viel Spaß!*

G

gentleman *der Herr (-en)*
(to) get (in/on) *einsteigen*
(to) get (out/off) *aussteigen*
(to) get (to) *kommen;* how do
  I get to . . .? *wie komme
  ich . . .?*
gladly *gern(e)*
glass *das Glas (¨er)*
(to) go *gehen*
good *gut*
goodbye *auf Wiedersehen*

H

half *halb*
(to) have *haben;* I'd like to
  have *ich hätte gern*

74 vierundsiebzig

here *hier*
hotel *das Hotel (-s)*
how? *wie?;* pardon? (what did
  you say?) *wie, bitte?*

I

I *ich*
if *wenn*
immediately *gleich*
in *in, im, in der*
intersection *die Kreuzung (-en)*
is *ist*
it *er, sie, es; ihn, sie, es*

J

jam, jelly *das Gelée (-s)
  die Konfitüre (-n)
  die Marmelade (-n)*
journey *die Fahrt (-en)*

K

key *der Schlüssel (-)*

L

lady *die Dame (-n);* ladies
  (toilet) *Damen*
lady (young) *das Fräulein (-)*
large *groß*
leaves (departs) *fährt . . . ab*
left *links;* turn to the left
  biegen Sie nach links! on
  the left side *auf der linken
  Seite*
lemon *die Zitrone (-n)*
letter *der Brief (-e)*
(to) lie (location) *liegen*
(to) like *mögen;* I would like
  . . . *ich möchte . . .* would
  you like . . .? *möchten Sie
  . . .?*
luggage *das Gepäck*

M

(to) make *machen;* that
  comes to . . . *das macht . . .*
man *der Herr (-en);* men
  (toilet) *Herren*
marketplace *der Marktplatz
  (¨e)*
match *das Streichholz (¨er)*

meal (set meal) *das Gedeck
(-e) das Menü (-s)*
menu *die Karte (-n)*
minute *die Minute (-n)*
Miss . . . *Fräulein . . .*
Mister (Mr.) . . . *Herr . . .*
Mrs. . . . *Frau . . .*
moment *der Moment (-e)*
more *mehr*
morning *der Morgen (-)*;
good morning! *guten
Morgen!*
much *viel*
my *mein, meine*

N
name *der Name (-n)*
nearest, next *nächste*
next door *nebenan*
night *die Nacht (-̈e)*
no (not any, none) *kein,
keine*
no (opposite of "yes") *nein*
not *nicht*
now *jetzt*
number *die Nummer (-n)*

O
o'clock *Uhr*; at eight o'clock
um acht Uhr
on *auf* (on horizontal surface)
an (on vertical surface, at the
edge of)
(to) open *öffnen*
open *offen*
opposite (across from)
gegenüber
or *oder*
orange juice *der Orangensaft*

P
pack, package *die Packung (-en)*
passport *der Paß(-̈sse)*
(to) pay *zahlen*
per (day) *pro (Tag)*
person *die Person (-en)*
pharmacy *die Apotheke (-n)*
piece *das Stück (-e)*
place, square *der Platz (-̈e)*
please *bitte*; yes, please? *bitte*

schön?
postcard *die Postkarte (-n)*
post office *die Post, das Postamt
(-̈er)*
pot (individual) *das Kännchen (-)*
powder *der Puder (-)*
premium (gas) *das Super*
(to) press *drücken*

R
regular (gas) *normal*
reserved *reserviert*
restaurant *das Restaurant (-s)*
right *rechts*; turn to the right
biegen Sie nach rechts! on the
right side *auf der rechten Seite*
room *das Zimmer (-)*; double
room *das Doppelzimmer*
single room *das Einzelzimmer*
rye (black) bread *das
Schwarzbrot (-e)*

S
sausage *die Wurst (-̈e)*
(to) say *sagen*; it says here
es steht hier
(to) see *sehen*
self service *die Selbstbedienung,
selbsttanken*
(to) serve *servieren*
shower *die Dusche (-n)*
side *die Seite (-n)*
(to) sign (document) *unterschreiben*
slow(ly) *langsam*
small *klein, kleine, kleines*
soap *die Seife (-n)*
(I'm) sorry *es (das) tut mir leid*
(to) speak *sprechen*
square (city) *der Platz (-̈e)*
stamp *die Briefmarke (-n)*
station *der Bahnhof (-̈e)*; main
station *der Hauptbahnhof*
stop (streetcar, etc.) *die
Station (-en), die Haltestelle
(-n)*
straight ahead *geradeaus*
street *die Straße (n)*
streetcar *die Straßenbahn (-en)*
subway *die U-bahn (-en), die
Untergrundbahn (-en)*

T

tart, flan *die Torte (-n)*
taxi *das Taxi (-s)*
taxi stand *der Taxistand (ˉe)*
tea *der Tee*
telephone *das Telefon (-e)*
thank (you) *danke*
(many) thanks *danke
    vielmals*
thanks (very much) *danke
    schön, schönen Dank*
the, that *der, die, das; den,
    die, das*
theater *das Theater (-)*
then *dann*
there *da, dort*
there is/are *es gibt*
this *dieser, diese, dieses;
    diesen, diese, dieses*
ticket *die Karte (-n), die
    Fahrkarte (train, bus),
    die Eintrittskarte (theater,
    zoo)*
till (until) *bis*
together *zusammen*
toilet *die Toilette (-n), das
    WC ("vay-tsay")*
to *nach (with place names)
    zu (specific locations)*
too *auch*
tooth brush *die Zahnbürste
    (-n)*
toothpaste *die Zahnkrem*
town, city *die Stadt (ˉe)*
track, platform (railroad)
    das Gleis (-e)
traffic lights *die Ampel (-n)*
train *der Zug (ˉe), der
    Personenzug (local), der
    Schnellzug (fast train,
    express)*
(to) transfer (bus, etc.)
    umsteigen; transfer here!
    steigen Sie hier um!
(to) travel, go *fahren;* when
    does the train go to . . . ?

*wann fährt der Zug nach
    . . . ?*
trip (journey) *die Fahrt (-en);*
    have a good trip! *gute
    Fahrt!*
(to) turn *abbiegen;* turn here!
    biegen Sie hier ab!

U

unfortunately *leider*
unoccupied *frei*
until (till) *bis*

V

very *sehr*

W

Waiter! *Herr Ober!*
Waitress (Miss)! *Fräulein!*
(to) want to *wollen*
we *wir*
what? *was?*
when? *wann?*
where *wo?*
which *welcher? welche?
    welches?; welchen?
    welche? welches?*
wife *die Frau (-en)*
wine *der Wein (-e)*
(to) wish/want *wünschen*
wish *der Wunsch (ˉe)*
with *mit*
wolf *der Wolf (ˉe)*
woman *die Frau (-en)*
workdays *werktags*

Y

you *Sie*
(to, for) you *Ihnen*
your *Ihr, Ihre, Ihres; Ihren,
    Ihre, Ihres*

Z

zoo *der Zoo (-s),
    Zoologischer Garten (ˉ)*

ITINERARY

DATE	PLACE

EXPENSES			
DATE	AMT.	U.S.$	FOR:

EXPENSES

DATE	AMT.	U.S.$	FOR:

EXPENSES			
DATE	AMT.	U.S. $	FOR:

PURCHASES

ITEM _____

WHERE BOUGHT _____

GIFT FOR _____ COST _____ U.S.$ _____

ITEM _____

WHERE BOUGHT _____

GIFT FOR _____ COST _____ U.S.$ _____

ITEM _____

WHERE BOUGHT _____

GIFT FOR _____ COST _____ U.S.$ _____

ITEM _____

WHERE BOUGHT _____

GIFT FOR _____ COST _____ U.S.$ _____

ITEM _____

WHERE BOUGHT _____

GIFT FOR _____ COST _____ U.S.$ _____

PURCHASES

ITEM _____

WHERE BOUGHT _____

GIFT FOR _____ COST _____ U.S.$ _____

ITEM _____

WHERE BOUGHT _____

GIFT FOR _____ COST _____ U.S.$ _____

ITEM _____

WHERE BOUGHT _____

GIFT FOR _____ COST _____ U.S.$ _____

ITEM _____

WHERE BOUGHT _____

GIFT FOR _____ COST _____ U.S.$ _____

ITEM _____

WHERE BOUGHT _____

GIFT FOR _____ COST _____ U.S.$ _____

PURCHASES

ITEM _____

WHERE BOUGHT _____

GIFT FOR _____COST_____U.S.$_____

ITEM _____

WHERE BOUGHT _____

GIFT FOR _____ COST_____U.S.$_____

ITEM _____

WHERE BOUGHT _____

GIFT FOR _____COST_____U.S.$_____

ITEM _____

WHERE BOUGHT _____

GIFT FOR _____COST_____U.S.$_____

ITEM _____

WHERE BOUGHT _____

GIFT FOR _____ COST_____U.S.$_____

ADDRESSES

NAME _____

ADDRESS _____

_____ PHONE _____

NAME _____

ADDRESS _____

_____ PHONE _____

NAME _____

ADDRESS _____

_____ PHONE _____

NAME _____

ADDRESS _____

_____ PHONE _____

NAME _____

ADDRESS _____

_____ PHONE _____

ADDRESSES

NAME _____

ADDRESS _____

_____ PHONE _____

NAME _____

ADDRESS _____

_____ PHONE _____

NAME _____

ADDRESS _____

_____ PHONE _____

NAME _____

ADDRESS _____

_____ PHONE _____

NAME _____

ADDRESS _____

_____ PHONE _____

ADDRESSES

NAME _____

ADDRESS _____

_____ PHONE _____

NAME _____

ADDRESS _____

_____ PHONE _____

NAME _____

ADDRESS _____

_____ PHONE _____

NAME _____

ADDRESS _____

_____ PHONE _____

NAME _____

ADDRESS _____

_____ PHONE _____

TRAVEL DIARY

DATE_____

DATE_____

DATE_____

DATE_____

DATE_____

DATE_____

DATE_____

TRAVEL DIARY

DATE_____

DATE_____

DATE_____

DATE_____

DATE_____

DATE_____

DATE_____

TRAVEL DIARY

DATE_____

DATE_____

DATE_____

DATE_____

DATE_____

DATE_____

DATE_____

MISCELLANEOUS